For all those men and women who are romantics at heart, and whose secret wish is to fall in love and live happily ever after.

How's Your Love Life?

♥

Merry Watson

Hale&Iremonger

Acknowledgements

Thank you to the following people for their loving support and encouragement: Les, Linda, Delia, Ross, David, Kate and Brian.

This book is dedicated to my husband, Leslie B. Watson.

© Merry Watson, 1992

This book is copyright. Apart from any fair dealing for the purpose of study, research, criticism, review or as otherwise permitted under the Copyright Act, no part may be reproduced by any process without written permission. Inquiries should be made to the publisher.

This expanded and revised edition typeset printed & bound by
Southwood Press Pty Limited
80-92 Chapel Street, Marrickville, NSW

For the publisher
Hale & Iremonger Pty Limited
GPO Box 2552, Sydney, NSW

National Library of Australia Cataloguing-in-Publication entry
Watson, Merry, 1958
How's Your Love Life?

ISBN   0 86806 499 8

1. Self-actualization (Psychology)
2. Interpersonal relations
3. Self-management (Psychology) 1. Title

Contents

Introduction	7
Part One	9

Background
Who This Book Is For
What You Will Gain
The 'Ideal' Relationship
  - What Does It Mean Anyway?
What's Your Choice?
What's It Going To Take?
    A Willingness To Do
    A Willingness To Try Something Different
Basic Principles
The Principles At Work

Part Two	19

Making It Real
Constructive Fantasising
How To Fantasise Constructively
Preparing To Fantasise
Exercise
What Your Fantasy Reveals About You
Exercise
Let Go Of The Past & Make Way For The New
Exercise
Forgiveness
The Benefits Of Forgiving
Exercise
Review

Part Three	43

Obstacles & How To Overcome Them
Are You Good Enough?
Exercise
Curing Loneliness

Building Your Self-Esteem
Forgive Yourself
Exercise
What's Special About Me?
Exercises
Treat Yourself To A Good Time
Exercise
Are You Ready & Willing?
What Does Love Mean, Anyway?
Exercise
Fears: Fact Or Fiction?
Positive Affirmations
Review

Part Four   67
Your Relationship Checklist
The Power Of List Writing
The Relationship Checklist
Checklist Categories
Isn't Love Enough?
Guidelines
Exercise
Your Relationship Together
Your Partner - Attitudes & Characteristics

Part Five   89
Next Steps
Commitment
Be Available
Circulate
Fantasise, Fantasise, Fantasise!
Be The Best You Can Be
Relax! & Love Yourself
Recommended Reading & Further Study

Introduction

For five years I worked in an introduction agency helping men and women find compatible companions or marriage partners.

From the beginning I was astonished that loneliness was so widespread: in the five years that I worked in the industry, we received over 20,000 enquiries from men and women of all ages, nationalities, backgrounds and occupations. That was just *one* agency in *one* city!

I interviewed hundreds and hundreds of "clients" and during that time I learned a great deal about the secret longings and fears of both men and women. Companionship, intimacy, love and marriage were central needs in their lives.

I also learned a lot about the matchmaking process: what people are looking for, how they go about looking, what works and what doesn't work in the search for a partner. Some of it was hilarious, some was tragic, some was heartwarming.

But I must confess that my interest in the dynamics of love and intimacy, companionship and marriage did not begin there.

It began with my own search for a perfect mate.

Although I never told anyone of my secret wish (I was too embarrassed to admit to such a fantasy), I always had a sense of what it would be like when I found the love of my life.

Then came a series of disastrous relationships! Reality struck, and I came down to earth with a thud! The truth was, I kept falling in love with men who didn't love me back, or attracting devoted souls who didn't interest me in the least! With bruised heart and battered ego I began to doubt my dream. Perhaps the perfect love I yearned for *did* only exist in romance novels and movies.

It took a failed marriage for my resolve to strengthen. If I couldn't have my dream relationship, then I'd rather spend the rest of my life single and unattached. I wasn't prepared to settle for second best, even if second best was reality.

I decided to give it everything I had to find the man of my dreams. I drew on my experience in the matchmaking business, my studies in psychology and my exploration into personal growth techniques including goal setting, relationships, self-esteem, personal effectiveness, visualisation and mind power.

Well, I did it! The man of my dreams is now my husband, and I've dedicated this book to him.

I was so obviously happy that friends started asking me how I did it. I told them. Surprise, surprise! It worked for them too!

So I thought I would write it all down, in case there were other unattached men and women out there who would find my techniques helpful and perhaps create that loving relationship they want for themselves.

Well, here it is. I hope you find it useful, and that you end up as happy and fulfilled in your dream relationship as I am in mine.

Merry Watson

Part One

Background

Background

Who This Book Is For

This book is for any adult, male or female, whose desire is to spend their life in an intimate love-filled relationship.

What You Will Gain

- Probably the best chance in your life so far of attracting the life partner of your choice
- More happiness than you've ever had before
- An end to loneliness
- A better understanding and appreciation of yourself and your needs when it comes to love
- Greater choice when it comes to relationships

The 'Ideal' Relationship — What Does It Mean Anyway?

I dedicated this book to my husband, but also to "men and women... whose secret wish is to fall in love and live happily ever after".

The "ideal" relationship will mean something different to everyone, of course. But the desire to experience that dizzy, wonderful falling-in-love feeling and the desire to live in harmony together seem to be two elements common to most people's understanding. I suppose this is as good a definition as any other of "ideal relationship".

For me, wanting an "ideal relationship" is about choosing to live my life as part of a couple. It means that I fulfill my life's purpose, achieve my goals, learn, grow, experience life's challenges and explore its possibilities all within the context of a lifetime partnership.

My ideal partner is the one who is there for me to go home to, someone who accepts me for who and what I am, and who loves me regardless! It is someone to share my fears, my hopes, my laughter and my tears, my errors and my triumphs. It is someone who thinks about me during the day, even when I am not around. It is someone who wants the best for me. It is someone who desires me, who admires me and who is proud to be with me - even when I'm scruffy or sick or just plain bad-tempered!

"Happily ever after" to me does not mean that we won't have disagreements or tough times. It means that the basic foundations of love, commitment, respect and trust remain intact whatever rocky or diamond-studded roads we travel as individuals or as a couple.

About that "falling in love" feeling... true, it isn't everything, and it may mellow into something more "warm and comfortable", but who would be without it in the beginning? It's a fabulous feeling - especially when it's mutual!

What does "ideal relationship" mean to you?

_____
_____
_____
_____
_____
_____
_____
_____
_____

What's Your Choice?

> *"There's no such thing as the perfect relationship."*
>
> *"You have to compromise in life."*
>
> *"All the good men/women are already taken."*
>
> *"Real relationships are never that easy."*
>
> *"Happily ever after only exists in books and movies."*
>
> *"Some people were never meant to marry."*
>
> *"There aren't enough men/women around. Someone has to miss out."*
>
> *"I just can't meet anyone suitable."*
>
> *"Men/women just want one thing."*
>
> *"Love is a matter of luck...and I am unlucky."*

Some people will use *any* excuse to get out of having a good relationship!

If you have ever voiced any of the opinions listed above, this is your point of choice and your challenge.

You can give up right now, close this book and give it to a friend.

Or you can turn the page, and with the help of this book... prove yourself wrong!

What's It Going To Take?

A Willingness To Do

Yes, this is one of those "How-To" books! It is a practical book, with exercises for you to do throughout so that you not only get an understanding of how to get more love into your life, but you actually start to do it!

It is based on the principle of "learning by doing". You have to do the work to see the results.

I used to be fascinated by these kinds of books. I would read every one I could get my hands on! But that's all I ever did. Just read. I never did the exercises. So nothing changed in my life. Sure, I knew all the theory, but I didn't do anything with it. I finally learned that understanding doesn't do it. Only the doing does it.

So if it's a real live in-the-flesh ideal relationship you want, rather than just a dream, please do the exercises! They are fun, and what you will learn and gain will be interesting and exciting.

To help you, I have provided some space throughout the book for you to make brief notes about your personal experience of the exercises.

There are also some exercises to which you will need to respond at length, so instead of writing in the book you will be using your own note paper.

These exercises are quite intensive, so take your time. Treat the book as a series of small meals rather than one large banquet. If you do read it straight through, I suggest you go back and do the exercises later at a leisurely pace. Give yourself the best possible chance of success!

A Willingness To Try Something Different

So far, you are not in the relationship of your dreams. It's going to take a willingness to try something new, different, unfamiliar and perhaps a little challenging in order to achieve an outcome which is different to past outcomes.

That means having a willingness to admit that perhaps the ways you have tried in the past don't work, and that doing something different will.

It's also going to take:

DESIRE - you have to really want it and admit to yourself that you do.

BELIEF - you must believe that it's possible.

ACCEPTANCE - you must be willing to receive it into your life.

CLARITY - you must be willing to decide exactly the kind of partner you want and the type of relationship you want.

You may be saying to yourself: *"Oh, no, this is going to be hard"*.

Yes, there is some work to be done by you.

Some of it will be different, even strange to you. This is a sure sign you are making headway!

Change is strange. That doesn't make it wrong. Like any new skill, what seems awkward at first soon becomes familiar and easy. Notice your doubts. And then do it anyway!

Ask yourself: *"Do I want this enough to do what it takes? How strong is my desire? How important is it to me to have a full, satisfying love life?"*

Keep your eyes, heart, mind and soul fixed on that dream to have a loving relationship with a wonderful partner, and take it one page at a time!

Basic Principles

The basic principles behind this book are not new. They are principles which I and many others have been using in all areas of life for many years with extraordinary results. For the purpose of this book the principles have been researched, collected, tested and applied specifically to the goal of creating the "ideal relationship".

So, here is a brief outline of the basic principles:

PERMISSION

It is okay to want an ideal relationship in your life - there is no right or wrong about it.

CHOICE

You can choose to have anything you want in your life - it's up to you.

RESPONSIBILITY

You can take responsibility for creating what you want in your life.

POWER

You have the power to bring whatever you want into your life.

OBSTACLES

Obstacles are those things which stand in the way of you having what you want in your life.

KNOWLEDGE

You already have all the information you need to get what you want - it's just a matter of learning how to tap into it.

CREATION

What you create in your life you first create in your mind.

SPECIFICITY

The more "fussy" and uncompromising you are about what you want, the more likely you are to get it.

Some of you will have come across these principles before.

Others of you may be scratching your heads, while still others of you may be asking *"Oh, really?"*

I am not going to devote the time and space to convince you that the principles are sound. It is not necessary to understand them, or even to agree with them! What *is* necessary is a willingness to check them out for yourself by doing the exercises. The important thing, in the end, is whether they work for you or not.

For those of you who would like a more in-depth understanding of the principles and techniques used, I have included a short reading list at the back of the book.

The Principles At Work

This is a broad outline of what to expect from the rest of the book.

In "Part Two - Making It Real" you will be fantasising! You will be letting your imagination go to dream up your ideal relationship, because being able to imagine actually being in your ideal relationship is a vital first step to making it a reality.

"Part Three - Obstacles & How To Overcome Them" is all about discovering and clearing away the obstacles that stand in the way of you having your ideal relationship. You will do this using various written exercises.

You will discover if you really *do* want an ideal relationship (or if you just *think* you do), what you want your relationship to be like, the probability of having it, how to increase your chances of having it, what some of your obstacles are and how to overcome them.

In "Part Four - Your Relationship Checklist" you will be writing a "shopping list" for your perfect partner. To do this you will be using all the information you have learned from Parts Two and Three.

"Part Five - Next Steps" outlines what to do after you have compiled your Relationship Checklist.

Now it's time to put the principles to work and see what they can do!

Part Two

Making It Real

Making It Real

What you create in your life you first create in your mind.

In this section you are going to create your ideal relationship in your mind.

You will be giving yourself permission to fantasise about a perfect Sunday spent with your ideal partner.

Constructive Fantasising

Fantasising is another word for *imagining* or *visualising*. Constructive fantasising is when you steer your imagination in the direction of a particular goal.

There are many ways to do it and everybody does it differently.

Some people, for example, can fantasise with their eyes open - this is usually called *daydreaming*. Daydreaming has often been frowned upon in the past as laziness or a waste of time, but it is becoming recognised as a very important and powerful part of the creation process.

Many people, when they close their eyes to fantasise, can "see" very clear pictures in their mind. Others may not see actual pictures at all, but fantasise by imagining *how it feels* to be in certain situations. Or they may be able to *hear* their fantasy in voices or sounds. It does not matter how you imagine. You may experience any combination of seeing, feeling and hearing.

There are many, many books and courses about fantasising, most often called *visualisation* (see page 96 for recommended reading).

How To Fantasise Constructively

Read through all the following instructions before beginning, so that once you commence the fantasising session you do not have to keep referring back to the book. It does not matter if you cannot remember everything you read in detail. The important thing is to get the general idea, then let your imagination take over.

Alternatively, you could record the instructions onto a tape and play it to yourself while you are fantasising. If you decide to do this, make sure you tape some lengthy pauses between each instruction (or be ready with the pause button) to give you time to let your imagination go. A series of three (...) dots indicates a pause.

Preparing To Fantasise

Get yourself comfortably upright in a chair, or on a bed (by yourself!) Only lie down if you are fairly sure you are not going to fall asleep -this exercise works best if you remain conscious!

Make sure you will not be disturbed for at least fifteen to twenty minutes.

Take in a slow, deep breath and let it out. Take in a second breath and at the same time close your eyes.

You are now ready to do some constructive fantasising.

EXERCISE

A Perfect Sunday

Follow these instructions as closely as you can, but don't worry if you stray a little, or you find it difficult in some spots. Just note it and move on to the next instruction.

Here we go...

You have your eyes closed and you are very relaxed... imagine that you are lying in bed very early on a Sunday morning, in the home you share with your ideal partner... who is sleeping beside you...

You open your eyes and you know that your partner is asleep beside you in the bed you share...look around the room... what can you see?... what do the walls look like?... what are the colours in the room?... how do the bed covers feel?... heavy?... feather light?... the light is just beginning to come into the room and you look towards the windows... notice the kind of drapes or coverings they have... can you hear any noises outside on this early Sunday morning?... birds?... children?... or is it very quiet?

Just lie there and get a sense of where you are and how you are feeling... knowing that your loving partner is lying beside you asleep in the bed...

...now your partner is waking up and turns to you... does he/she reach for you?... do you cuddle?... do you talk?... laugh?... just take a few minutes to notice how the two of you are together on this wonderful Sunday morning...

...now it is time to get up and do all those bathroom things... as you get out of bed, notice what you are wearing... what your partner is wearing... and what happens... do you go to the bathroom together, or take turns?... is it silent, or do you put music on?... what kind of noises are there?... do you chatter?... do you touch one another?... giggle and tease perhaps?... take a few minutes to go through the bathroom chores...

...now it is time to have breakfast... where in your home do you eat your Sunday morning breakfast?... what time is it?... how does your breakfast area look? ... sunny?... cosy?... quiet?... what sounds can you hear?... clock?... music?... birds?... wind in the trees?... notice where you are, what you are feeling, seeing, hearing, doing...

...what do you have for breakfast?... do you and your partner eat the same things?... or do you have different tastes?... who cooks?... do you do it together?... does one of you read the paper?... who makes coffee or tea?... how does it feel preparing

breakfast together?... is there laughter... touching... or quiet intimacy?... who does most of the talking?... do you talk at all?... take a few minutes to imagine preparing breakfast together...

...where do you sit down to eat in your home?... outdoors... at a breakfast bar?... lounge-room sofa?... dining table?... is there anyone else around, or are you alone together?... what are the feelings between you as you eat breakfast together?... what happens?... imagine the sights and sounds and feelings...

...breakfast is over now... and your partner has to leave the house for a few minutes... perhaps to go to the corner store or get some fresh air... as you hear the door close behind him/her, you sit by yourself... and you think about your relationship... how do you feel about your partner?... how does your partner feel about you?... what lovely memories do you share?... look around the room and see evidence of your partner in your home... books, magazines, belongings...

...you hear the key in the door as your partner returns... you don't look around... he/she comes up behind you... does your partner grab you from behind?... are there kisses and touching?... or do you joke and kid around?... or is yours a quiet, peaceful silence?...

...now you sit down together to plan what you are going to do with your perfect Sunday... do you sit together or opposite one another?.. do you touch?... who does most of the talking?... what do you decide to do today?... spend it together or go your separate ways to pursue your own interests?... slob around at home?... visit friends?... have friends over?... spend it with children?... with nature?... playing sport?... who decides?... perhaps you don't discuss it... you just blend into the day... take a few minutes to imagine planning your Sunday together...

...now it is lunchtime on your perfect Sunday together... where are you?... what are you doing?... are you together?... how do you

feel?... is it quiet or noisy?... is there laughter?... what do you eat for lunch?... take a few minutes to imagine having lunch...

...now it's the end of the day and you are having dinner together... or with friends... where are you and what are you doing in the evening of this perfect day?... take a few minutes to experience your late afternoon, sunset, twilight into the dark...

...now you are back where you began the day... lying beside your loved one in bed... who has fallen asleep beside you... how did you say good night to each other?... you lie there looking into the darkened room... look around... how is it different to the morning?... what noises can you hear now?... frogs?... traffic?... and how are you feeling after you have spent a perfect Sunday with your partner?... tired?... excited?... happy?... fulfilled?... think about your partner lying there beside you... can you hear breathing?... can you see the outline of your partner's body?... can you feel his/her warmth?...

...take a few minutes to review the day you have spent... how did it feel?... what images come to mind?... how were you together?... was it filled with fun?... laughter?... peace?... excitement?... warmth?... love making?... cosiness?... did you fight or disagree?... did you talk a lot?... touch a lot?...

... now you are beginning to fall asleep... do you feel safe?... contented?... you drift deeper into sleep... sleep...

... now it's time to come out of your fantasy... become aware of what you are sitting on and the room you are in... notice your breathing... hear the sounds around you... and open your eyes!

The point of the constructive fantasising exercise is to get you to imagine how it will feel to be in your ideal relationship doing every-day activities together.

Many people long to be loved, but cannot *really* imagine what it would be like on a day-to-day basis to actually be with that person.

This exercise begins to make it real in your *mind*, which is an essential step to making it real in your *life*.

Did you find it easy or difficult to do? Did it seem "real" to you? Could you imagine being in this situation with this ideal person? What was particularly vivid to you (feelings, sights, sounds, events)?

Notes: _____

_____
_____
_____
_____
_____
_____
_____
_____
_____
_____

The more "real" it seemed the better, because your relationship will consist of much more than the falling in love part, or sex, or kissing... it will consist of living together from day to day, going through all kinds of ordinary, as well as extraordinary, experiences together.

The more you can imagine these everyday experiences and the more often you can constructively fantasise about them, the more powerful will be your ability to create this relationship as a reality in your life.

Constructive fantasising is something you can do often. You can repeat the *Perfect Sunday* exercise, or you can make up your own using other everyday situations you may find yourselves in: being at work and your partner phoning you or calling to take you to lunch... what happens on a typical weekday morning... your wedding... going on holiday together... being with friends... going to the movies... being with children (perhaps your own)... being outdoors... going shopping together...

Constructive fantasies can include any activity that you do in your life already, but now you include your partner. It is very important that you make mental room in your life for him or her. If you can't make room in your mind, the chances of making room in your life are very small.

What Your Fantasy Reveals About You

Taking a closer look at what happens in your fantasy can also give you a lot of information about yourself, the way you are thinking, and your "chances" of actually having that ideal relationship at this stage of your life.

You now have the opportunity to begin discovering, from taking a close look at your constructive fantasising, some of your positive and negatives beliefs about relationships.

We all have some beliefs about relationships which are positive, and some which are negative.

An example of a positive belief would be : *"Being in love means two people care about each other"*.

A negative belief would be: *"Love hurts"*.

Our beliefs come from the past. They are things we have made decisions about based on our own past experiences (good and bad), or things we have learned from other people (such as our parents, when we were growing up).

These beliefs can help us go forward in life, or they can hold us back.

The tricky bit is that often we do not even know what these beliefs actually are. They often have become such a part of us that they seem like *truth* or *fact*.

The good news is that we can discover what these beliefs are, and then we can decide to keep them or throw them away. The ones you will want to keep will be those that contribute to happy, successful relationships. The ones you will want to discard will be the destructive beliefs.

EXERCISE

Think back over your *Perfect Sunday* fantasy and answer the following questions:

1. At any time during the fantasy, did your "ideal partner" take on the form of someone from your past?

Many men and women who have tried this kind of constructive fantasising at some point in the process imagine that their ideal partner is someone from their past. A previous lover or spouse, for example.

In some ways this is quite natural. You may have actually experienced some of the fantasised situations with a real person in the past. This is fine, especially if that experience was a pleasant one. So if you have a memory of, say, cooking breakfast with a past lover that was wonderful and that's the quality of "cooking breakfast" you want to experience in the future, that's great!

However, if a *past* lover or spouse keeps popping up in place of your *future* ideal partner, it is possible that you haven't completely let go of that old relationship. You may not have even seen that person for many years. But perhaps you are still angry, or hurt, or still feel guilty about that relationship. Or perhaps you still "carry a torch" for that person. This is a sure sign that you are holding on to the past, and this can only keep you from moving into the future.

It is important to let go of the old if you want to move on to the new. It you still hold negative feelings about past relationships, those feelings can affect future relationships. You may find yourself with a pattern or a series of relationships that leave you feeling the same way...abandoned, abused, rejected, used, guilty etc.

Now is a good time to let go of those old relationships. Even if you feel that you *have* let go, do the following exercise for each person from your past who appeared in your constructive fantasy.

Let Go Of The Past & Make Way For The New

Write down the names of anyone from your past who appeared as your "ideal partner" in your fantasy (there may have been more than one).

_____

_____

_____

You are going to do another constructive fantasy so that you can let go of each of these past relationships.

Prepare yourself for a constructive fantasy session as you did the first time (see "Preparing To Fantasise").

EXERCISE

Completion Fantasy

Imagine that you are walking along a path... and coming towards you is this person from your past... you walk towards each other and stop in front of each other... about a metre apart... you look at this person, taking in the sight, sound and sense of him/her... you notice that you are connected to each other by a rope which is about a metre long... you look into this person's eyes, and communicate to him/her anything you wish to communicate... you may talk... or perhaps that person can feel your thoughts... say anything you wish to say... these may be positive... or negative... say everything you wish to say... take a few minutes...

...thank this person for the experience of knowing them... and tell him/her that you are letting them go... that they are free... then take a pair of scissors from your back pocket... or perhaps from a bag you carry... and cut the rope that has joined you... keep cutting until the rope is completely severed... keep cutting... then tell this person good-bye in any way that seems correct to you... then turn and begin to walk away from this person... perhaps you stop and look back... and you see this person surrounded by brilliant white light... you turn away again and continue back along your path... towards a beautiful white light of your own... you know that your future partner and a life of love is waiting for you at the end of the path in the white light...

...bring your awareness back to your surroundings... breathe deeply... and open your eyes!

People often feel emotional over this exercise. Others find it difficult to sever the "tie" that joins them - they have trouble letting go.

Perhaps you feel sad yet complete, as if something is over. Perhaps you feel a sense of relief. You may feel surprised that you still felt emotional about someone from your past. Were you shocked at some of the things you said to this person? This is all information for you about the way you have been thinking about relationships, yours in particular. For example, do you *want* to let go of that past relationship?

The important thing is that you have taken a big step towards being free and available for a new relationship.

Repeat this exercise with each of the people on your list. You will find some easier than others. If you find that you cannot break the tie completely (perhaps it is still hanging by a thread), do the exercise again until you can sever it completely.

If difficulties persist, or you still feel as if you haven't really let go, try one or both of the following:

. Contact that person in real life and *sort it out*, whether that means apologising for some wrong, giving the relationship a second chance, or whatever. Perhaps you still have a secret hope that the relationship is the right one for you. You need to find out so that you can go forward in your life, instead of being stuck in the past.

. Do the *Forgiveness Exercise* (see page 40) with this person. This is especially useful if it is impossible to contact the person in real life for physical or emotional reasons. It is a marvellous exercise if you still have a lot of unfinished communication to express (grief, anger, resentment, guilt).

This may seem like a lot of work. But the rewards are worth the effort. You may begin to feel light and free for the first time in years, as you begin to release the pain from past relationships. And this can only be good for your future "ideal" relationship, which you want to be happy, and long lasting.

Notes: _____

_____
_____
_____
_____
_____
_____
_____
_____
_____

2. Were there places in the fantasy you had difficulty imagining?

You may have had difficulty imagining certain parts of the fantasy. You may even have had difficulty imagining *any* of it.

If you had difficulty with the whole exercise, this could be for a number of different reasons:

- Lack of real-life experience in relationships. This would result in you having limited information about relationships on which your imagination can draw.
- You are unable to think beyond either the desire for a relationship, or beyond the "falling in love" part of a relationship. The day-to-day is not real for you.

You may need more information about relationships.

You can do this in a number of ways: talk to friends who are in happy relationships and find out how it feels for them, or you can get some more experience for yourself by going out with more potential partners, going on more dates, talking with and socialising with people in general. Find out what you like and what you don't like. Perhaps you just need more general relationship experience.

Perhaps your past relationships have been so disastrous that you can't imagine a happy one!

Or perhaps you have just never given it much thought before - having a wonderful relationship has seemed so remote to you that you haven't even bothered to imagine what it might be like.

Perhaps it hurts too much to think about something you don't think you can have.

Perhaps you have thought that once you fall in love with someone and they love you back, you don't have to worry about what happens next. Many romance novels *end* at this point, and if you have limited personal experience of relationships it is easy to get hooked into the "happily ever after" notion.

True, you *can* live happily ever after, but you need to do it beyond the first kiss... you need to live happily ever after eating, sleeping, working, washing socks...

If you *do* want to be in a happy relationship, but you are unable to imagine it, it is possible that you may have some beliefs that are contradicting each other.

For example, one of your beliefs may be :*"I want to be in a loving, lasting relationship"* but you may have another belief *"I'm not sure that I'm good enough for someone"*. Or *"I really want someone to love me (but) I am afraid of getting hurt (again)."*

Conflicting beliefs will create a blockage. The beliefs will "battle it out", causing confusion and often pain and unhappiness. What they surely *won't* create is your ideal relationship!

We will take a look at conflicting beliefs a little later in the book: discovering what they are and what to do about them.

Notes: _____

_____
_____
_____
_____
_____
_____
_____
_____
_____

3. Did your fantasy go wrong in places? Did it contain unpleasant experiences?

Perhaps everything was going along fine until you were making breakfast together and an argument broke out about who was going to do the dishes... or your partner went silent on you when you wanted to talk... or you felt terribly lonely even though you were with your so-called "ideal partner".

If your fantasy "turned sour" at some point, it is most likely reflecting some past real-life unpleasant experience in a previous relationship, either your own or of a role model (parents or others close to you). Perhaps you and your ex-spouse used to fight in the kitchen all the time. Perhaps your mother got the silent treatment from your father, or you yourself did from a past lover, for example.

This is very useful information about your expectations of

relationships, because it is possible that you will re-create those unpleasant experiences in future relationships, even if you don't consciously wish to do so. Have you ever had two relationships or more in a row where the same kind of problem kept popping up, such as jealousy, arguments, unfaithfulness, violence?

These destructive cycles can be broken, and awareness is the first step. You have already taken that step by doing the exercises outlined so far.

More serious patterns, such as violence or abuse, may require professional counselling and support to assist you in healing these past hurts.

But there is a great deal you can do for *yourself* to change the pattern of unhappy relationships.

Firstly, you can do the *Forgiveness Exercise* for each past relationship in which you suffered hurt or unpleasant experiences. The instructions for this exercise appear at the end of this section, and it is an extraordinarily powerful way of discovering buried hurts and healing them, thus freeing you to move on to healthy, happy relationships.

Secondly, you can repeat the constructive fantasy exercise *A Perfect Sunday* (as many times as you wish) and each time the unpleasant incident occurs, *freeze the action!* Go back a step or two and re-imagine it *the way you want it to be*. Keep doing this until the unwanted image goes away. For example, if you and your ideal partner are arguing over breakfast, *stop* and take it back a scene or two and *re-shoot the scene*, this time having the two of you *kissing* over breakfast instead!

You can practise this re-shooting technique by imagining you are looking at a wall. What colour is it? Okay, now *change the colour*. If it won't change, keep trying. Throw the wall out and get a new one. Now give it stripes. Now spots. Get the idea?

36 How's Your Love Life?

You are in control of what goes on in your mind. You have the power to create it any way you want.

For some people, difficulty with this technique reflects a feeling that they have little or no control over what happens to themselves or their lives. Life happens *to* them. They feel as if circumstances carry them along.

If you are one of these people, practising this re-shooting technique can help you actually gain more control over your real day-to-day existence.

Thirdly, you can move on to the next section in this book where you will be discovering those obstacles which get in the way of you having the ideal relationship you want, and where you will have the opportunity to re-shape those patterns and beliefs - first in your mind, then in your life.

Notes: _____

4. **Did your mind drift off in another direction? Did you stop following the instructions during the fantasising?**

This can be good! If you still kept to the general theme - which was spending Sunday with your ideal partner - then the fact that you went off on an individual tangent is good! You probably have a very clear, strong idea of how you would spend your Sunday - and it was obviously different from mine, or anybody else's! You are off to a great start in creating your ideal relationship.

However, if you drifted off the subject altogether (if you started thinking about work, or visiting your mother, for example) then this is a good alarm bell!

Again, you are receiving very useful information from your own mind.

Perhaps you cannot really imagine being with your ideal partner. Or it's possible that, while *in theory* you want an ideal relationship, there is something about it that bothers you. You may have conflicting intentions and we will be exploring this in the next section of the book.

If you did drift off to another subject, what you drifted off *to* could be a key to something that is standing in the way of you having the relationship you want.

For example, if you started thinking about work, then perhaps something about your work is an obstacle (are you concerned that a relationship will take you away from your career? your independence?). Or if you started thinking about your mother, perhaps you have a concern about her influence/opinion/welfare if you became seriously involved with someone. If you started thinking about your children, perhaps you have concerns about the effects of a new partner on them. If you started thinking about your body (how fat/ugly/badly clothed you think you are) perhaps you believe you have to be perfect before you can have the relationship you want.

Also look at what *part* of the fantasy you drifted off. If, for example, your mind drifted off during the "bedroom scene", perhaps you have some concerns or anxieties about the sexual part of relationships. Or touching. Or having intimate conversations.

Get the idea? Your mind will give you all kinds of information when you are fantasising - useful information about the way you think and act, information that you can work with and use to get you closer to the type of relationship you want.

Notes: _____
_____
_____
_____
_____
_____

Forgiveness

If there are incidences from the past that you are still mentally or emotionally "holding on to", this exercise can work wonders.

If there are people from your past you are still angry or upset with, this exercise will help you let that go and get on with a happier future.

If there are past relationships that continue to make you feel sad when you think about them, or past lovers you still have an attachment to, this exercise will help you to put them behind you.

How do you feel about forgiving wrongs done to you in the past? When I have recommended this exercise to people in the past, there have been mixed reactions.

Some people are astonished when they realise that they are holding a grudge.

Others even feel angry. *Why should I forgive them?* they ask. *I'll never be able to forgive them for what they did to me.*

Still others don't understand what there is to forgive. They say they are not angry, just sad.

The Benefits Of Forgiving

The *Forgiveness Exercise* is done for *your* benefit, not for the benefit of the person or incident to be forgiven.

It frees you from fantasising about the past, which *no* amount of fantasising will change! If you often cast your mind back to that unhappy failed relationship or the time you were hurt or betrayed, how can your mind, heart, soul and body be free to experience a fresh, potentially happy future? Your mind is still caught up in the past.

Even if you don't *think* you are angry, or that there is anything to forgive at all, you may be surprised. Often we bury anger or resentment deep down inside us, because we think it is wrong or unacceptable to feel these emotions towards others.

Or we take the blame onto ourselves. We see it as our own fault that the relationships failed. We berate ourselves over and over with *"I should have done that...I shouldn't have done this..."*

If you feel guilty about a past relationship, especially if you think you have hurt someone else (maybe *you* left someone broken - hearted), then the chances are that you are angry with yourself. In fact, if you are angry with someone else, you are probably also angry with *yourself* for being taken advantage of! In both cases, do the *Forgiveness Exercise* with yourself. (See section on "Building Your Self-Esteem".)

Take a few minutes to think about those people in your life with whom you associate some hurt or anger, and write down their names.

Notes: _____

_____
_____
_____
_____
_____
_____

EXERCISE

"I Forgive You"

Take an exercise book, or several sheets of paper. Make sure you have two pages lying side by side, or two facing pages open in your exercise book.

Choose someone from the past with whom you associate some kind of hurt (an ex-spouse or lover, for example). Note that you don't have to *want* to forgive this person in order to achieve benefit from this exercise. The exercise is for your own progress towards a happy healthy relationship in the future.

You may indeed end up forgiving this person, and that's terrific if it happens. However, that is not the primary goal here.

You will need a pen or pencil and about 30 minutes of privacy.

You will be writing repeatedly the same sentence down the left hand page. On the right hand page you will be noting your *reactions* to the statement on the left: thoughts, emotions, even physical sensations. Write anything that comes to you. No-one else is ever going to read what you write, and the more honest you can be with yourself the better the result will be.

The statement you will be writing repeatedly on the left hand page is

I,(your name), forgive (the person's name) completely.

(For example, *I, Merry, forgive John completely.*)

Keep writing this same statement over and over, followed by your reactions on the right hand page.

What will be happening is that if you do not agree with the statement (*to forgive*), you will begin reacting against it. It may not be in thoughts, and it may not happen immediately. You may get no reaction to start with. But if you keep writing this forgiveness line, you will begin to stir up any negative feelings you may not even have been aware you had about that person. You may recall incidences that you had forgotten.

It's possible to go through a whole range of thoughts and feelings while doing this exercise: sorrow, anger, guilt, remorse, understanding - even forgiveness, love and compassion, eventually! Keep going until you have got it all out of your system concerning that person. How long will that take? *As long as it takes!* You may need to write the forgiveness statement fifty times or five hundred times. You can do it all in one go, or break it down over a few days. You will know when you are done - there will be no more emotional reactions left.

Repeat this forgiveness exercise with any other relationship that has affected you deeply in the past.

By pouring out your feelings on paper rather than to the person's face, you avoid harming anyone (including *yourself*).

The point here is to *heal* the past, not to rip open the wound and make a few more cuts!

After completing this exercise you may feel a wonderful sense of calm, relief and peace, although you may also be surprised at the intensity of emotions you may have felt during the process.

You have been constructively facing the pain of the past, and this will allow you to let it go.

Destroy the notes from your forgiveness exercises. You can shred them, burn them or toss them out as a symbol of your decision to let go of these attachments to the past - once and for all!

Review

Phew! You have already put a lot of effort towards creating your ideal relationship, believe it or not.

In doing the exercises set so far, you have begun to make your future relationship real by creating it in your mind through constructive fantasising. You have let go of past hurts and past relationships through the *Completion Exercise* and the *Forgiveness Exercise* so that you can be free for the new relationship to come into your life.

You have also had a glimpse at some of the *Obstacles* that may be standing in the way of you having the relationship of your dreams.

In the next section of the book you will be exploring those obstacles and clearing them away, leaving you with more choice than ever before when it comes to creating a happy, healthy relationship.

Part Three

Obstacles & How To Overcome Them

Obstacles & How To Overcome Them

So, what do you *really* want? What is your true intention when it comes to your love life?

Does that sound like a silly question considering that you are probably reading this book to help you find the ideal partner?

Well, it's *not* such a silly question.

We often have beliefs and habits which get in the way of us having what we want for ourselves.

A young man at a dance badly wants to dance with a particular girl he has seen across the room, but he believes he will be rejected. So he does not ask, and he misses out. His *desire* is to dance with the girl. His *belief* is that he will be rejected because he is not good enough.

It is possible to have conflicting beliefs when it comes to wanting an ideal relationship. On the one hand we want to be happy in a lasting, fulfilling relationship, but on the other hand...

No, no, not me! I hear some of you say. I *really* want to be in a wonderful relationship! It's the most important thing to me!

Welcome to a very revealing section of this book!

The beliefs behind the success or failure of our love life are often subtle because we have had them so long that they seem part of us.

Our beliefs about ourselves and about relationships begin forming at a very early age.

Our first lessons about marriage, for example, were learned from observing our parents, or the adults who took care of us as children. The way our mother and father related to each other would have set up a "model" against which we measure our own adult relationships.

Even when as adults we can make up our own minds about what is right and wrong for us, there is often still an unconscious tendency to abide by those very early beliefs. No doubt you have heard how children of alcoholic parents or abusive parents unwittingly marry or become involved with alcoholic or abusive partners, even when they had vowed never to do so.

We will be looking at the beliefs you have which directly affect your love life: beliefs about yourself, about relationships, commitment, marriage, children, sex, trust, etc.

Look at the exercises as a fun, interesting exploration of what goes on inside your head. Don't judge yourself along the way. Be kind to yourself. The important thing is to keep those values and intentions which are compatible with what you want and to let go of those which are *not*.

Are You Good Enough?

Do you deserve to have the ideal relationship?
Do you believe it's possible for you to be lucky in love?
Are you good enough for someone to love passionately?
Are you special?
Are you lovable?
Do you believe you are perfect for someone just as you are?
Do you deserve the best life has to offer when it comes to love?
Could someone be blissfully happy spending the rest of their life with you?

The Bible says *"Love your neighbour as yourself"* (Lev 19:18). Many people don't love *themselves* very much at all. Many people would have happier lives if they treated themselves even *half* as well as they treat their neighbour!

Self-esteem, the ability to like and love yourself, is the foundation of attracting a healthy relationship and keeping it healthy. If

Obstacles & How To Overcome Them

you don't love, respect or care for yourself, why should someone else?

EXERCISE

Play around with some of the above phrases, and find out what you really think of yourself. Write the phrases as if they were true:

I, (your name), deserve to have the ideal relationship.

I, ..., am good enough for someone to love passionately.

I, ..., am special.

I, ..., am lovable.

I, ..., am perfect for someone just the way I am.

I, ..., deserve the best of love.

Similar to the technique in the *Forgiveness Exercise*, write one of the phrases on the left hand page, and note your reactions on the right hand page. Any beliefs you have which contradict the statement will surface. Keep going until there are no negative thoughts left to write.

You won't have to work through many of the phrases before you have a good idea of your level of self-esteem!

Some of the many negative beliefs you uncover may include: *"No, I don't deserve it... I'm too ugly... too stupid... I failed in my first marriage, why should I deserve a second chance?... I'm no good at relationships... no-one has ever loved me and no one ever will... I'm too ordinary... only smart/intelligent/beautiful/rich/independent/educated people have wonderful relationships"* etc.

You may have experienced all kinds of emotions while doing these exercises. Perhaps you felt sad and sorry for yourself... or amazed that you dislike or even hate yourself... or angry and resentful that you don't have the love that you want in your life. This is all good information.

Believing that you deserve to be loved is vital for attracting the love you want and keeping that love alive and flourishing once you are in a relationship.

If you don't think you are worthy or good enough or deserving enough or attractive enough...guess what? You are likely to attract partners who will agree with you!

What's the point of attracting a partner at all if the relationship itself is going to be short-lived or hurtful?

It is here, in the area of self-esteem, where you lay the foundations for a healthy, happy relationship.

There are lots of things you can do to build your self-esteem, and some of these are described a little later in the book.

But first let's look at another area also affected by low self-image.

Curing Loneliness

Working in an introduction agency for five years, I was shocked to discover what a widespread problem *loneliness* is in our society.

Many, if not most, of the people who came to the introduction agency to meet a potential partner were lonely. They believed that meeting the right partner would cure their loneliness. All they needed was a loving companion, and *everything would be all right*.

True, sharing your life with a loving partner *can* be wonderful!

But no loving partner can convince you that you are desirable and special and lovable if you don't believe it yourself.

Having someone to love you begins with *you* loving you.

Otherwise you could be constantly worried that your partner will find out what you, deep down, believe to be true: that you are not good enough, or worthy of being loved, or special.

In fact, self-esteem can be so low that when someone falls in love with you, you regard them with suspicion! The only really effective way to beat loneliness is to become your own best friend. Only *you* can make you happy.

So curing loneliness begins with building your self-esteem. You know for sure that *you* are never going to leave you!

You may have learned as a child that "loving yourself" was wrong. This is common. I remember at school how important it was not to be a "big head": the ultimate insult was *"oh, you love yourself"* or *"you are up yourself"*!

People with low self-esteem criticise and blame themselves all the time, either out loud or in their own heads. They mentally "beat themselves up" over and over again. Listen to yourself once in a while. How many times do you say to yourself things like: *"It's all my fault... oh, I'm so stupid... why did I do that?... I'm so ugly... I hate my body... I'm not attractive enough..."*?

People with low self-esteem are lonely. How can you criticise and bully yourself all the time and still feel secure, loved and as if you are wanted?

Building Your Self-Esteem

I have a five-year-old daughter. I love her very much, and I would never intentionally hurt her or be unkind to her.

One day I had a startling realisation. If I would not intentionally say hurtful or critical things to my own daughter, why would I say them to myself? Would I ever tell her that she was ugly, or fat, or stupid, or unlovable? Of course not - she would be devastated! And yet here I was devastating *myself*!

These days I try to treat myself as if I were my own daughter. This means that I discipline myself and correct myself, but it also means that I forgive myself, comfort myself, praise myself and even hug myself - just as I would do to my own daughter.

Perhaps you would like to try treating yourself as if you were your own child.

In being more loving and forgiving of yourself, you will become more loving and forgiving of other people. And that is a sure way of attracting more love (in all ways) into your life!

Forgive Yourself

When something goes wrong, often the first person we blame is ourselves. We punish ourselves.

If we received a lot of criticism and blame as children, when we leave home and become "grown ups" we often take over our parents' critical function and start *judging, criticising and rejecting* ourselves!

We think we are bad when we make mistakes. We give ourselves a hard time if we "muck up". This becomes a habit, until we are constantly criticising ourselves for being "wrong".

Perhaps it's time to forgive yourself for all your own "wrongs".

EXERCISE

If you have not already done so, do the *Forgiveness Exercise* (described on page 40) with yourself.

I, (your name), forgive myself completely.

Discover what you have been holding against yourself. This is important. Would you hold a grudge against your own child for something it did "wrong" in the past? So why do it to *yourself*?

If you hate yourself, how are you going to be able to accept someone loving you? You probably won't believe them - how could anyone love someone as terrible as *you* ?

Keep up the exercise for as long as it takes you to begin reacting with compassion, understanding and love towards yourself.

When I did this exercise, it took me a whole week of writing the "forgiveness" statement at least seventy times a day to reach that point! But it felt wonderful by the end. I actually shed tears of remorse at how badly I had been punishing myself for imagined "wrongs" all of my life! Then I had to forgive myself for feeling so guilty about *that* !

You can continue to forgive yourself on an ongoing basis, each day, as you continue to make the inevitable mistakes of your life. Make the mistake, point it out to yourself, tick yourself off (if you must), then forgive yourself and let the incident go. Apart from any other benefits, you will save so much time and energy when you are no longer going over and over your mistakes!

Once you have reached a point where you can be understanding, compassionate, forgiving and loving to yourself it becomes much less important what others think of you. That will mean that you will feel good about yourself around others. When you feel good about yourself, you tend to be good to others as well. This has the effect of other people liking you and wanting to be around you more. People are attracted to you. You receive more love.

What's Special About Me?

Believing that there are special and lovable things about yourself is important if you are to believe that someone will love you enough to want to be in a relationship with you, or spend the rest of their life with you.

EXERCISE

Sit down and write out a list of all your positive qualities, all the things that you like about yourself.

List everything you can think of, from *"nice eyebrows"* to *"make good cups of tea"* to *"honest, kind and a good listener"*. Describe yourself, but only your good points. If you find yourself listing criticisms, *stop!*

If you cannot think of many good qualities, ask your friends what they see as your strengths.

Notes: _____

_____

_____

_____

_____

_____

From your notes, write a comprehensive list on a loose sheet of paper. Pin it up where you can see it often, so that during those time when you are being hard on yourself, you can remind yourself that you are not so bad after all!

Write a list of everything you have to offer in a relationship.

Notes: _____

_____

_____

_____

_____

_____

This list will be similar to the list in the above exercise, but it may prompt you to think of some good qualities which are specific to being with another person in a committed relationship, such as *trust, faithfulness, loyalty...* even *the ability to have children* is a positive quality!

If your mind keeps drifting off to things you *don't* like about yourself, or the things you have *not* got to offer a relationship, keep a note of these on a separate piece of paper.

Later on you can take an honest look at this list and decide which of these things are just your exaggerated criticisms of yourself, and which could do with some genuine improvement.

As a good double-check, ask a trusted friend for an honest opinion. This takes courage, but if you want to make the most of yourself, it pays to know if there are simple improvements you can make to yourself, or if you are worrying about nothing.

EXERCISE

"I Love You"

Sit down quietly in front of a mirror and talk to yourself. Get to know and appreciate yourself.

At first you will probably feel silly. Then you will probably start picking yourself to pieces *("oh, look at those lines")*. You may even dislike looking at yourself at all!

(When I first started doing this exercise, I put it off and put it off. I think I was actually afraid to look at myself - that's how healthy *my* self-esteem was!)

Smile at yourself. Say hello.

Say your name out loud.

Tell yourself to your face what a nice person you are.

Read aloud from your lists of special qualities.

Look into your own reflected eyes and tell yourself how this exercise makes you feel.

Say *"I love you"* to your reflection.

Tell yourself that you approve of yourself and will be kinder to yourself in the future.

Practise this exercise regularly, every day if you can... or just quickly say *"hello"* to yourself as you pass a mirror.

You may resist doing this. That's a good sign - what you are resisting is probably exactly what you need to do. You are probably just not accustomed to being so nice to yourself! Go ahead - being kind to yourself can only do you good.

Treat Yourself To A Good Time

Are you the sort of person who is always doing nice things for other people?

When was the last time you did some nice things for yourself?

As well as giving yourself nice words, there are other ways to be kind to yourself.

EXERCISE

Do at least one nice thing for yourself every day.

Here is a list of simple, loving actions you can do for yourself. (There's no excuse for not trying some of these - most take little or no extra money or time!)

Write yourself a "thank you" note for whatever is special about you

Buy yourself some flowers, just for being you

Pat yourself on the back

Buy a packet of "well done" or "excellent" stickers (the kind they give kids at school) and reward yourself

Encourage yourself with a hug (yes, that's right! Wrap your arms around yourself and give yourself a squeeze!)

Pat yourself on the head and say *"Good girl/good boy!"*

Give yourself a wink as you pass a mirror

Once you try a few of these and see how wonderful they make you feel, I am sure you will think up a few of your own!

Are You Ready & Willing?

Would you be ready if you ideal partner turned up in your life tomorrow?

Think about it!

What immediately comes to mind will be all those areas of your life which

- you want to "tidy up" before you are truly ready for the relationship of your dreams to walk into your life, or
- you *think* you need to be different before the relationship of your dreams will walk into your life

Examples of areas which you might like to "tidy up" in your life could be a relationship that you have not bothered to finish properly, such as that divorce you could have got three years ago, or that casual relationship you continue just to ease your loneliness.

Examples of something you may believe needs to be different before you get the relationship of your dreams would be: lose weight, be financially secure, have your career established, have nicer underwear!

Be as ready as you can! Complete those old relationships and make the most of yourself and your surroundings. Be the best person you can be.

In the meantime, don't be too hard on yourself! A loving partner is one who supports and encourages you to become the best you can be, but a loving partner is also someone who loves you, not for your potential, but for who you are already. Besides, if you wait until you are perfect - it may never happen!

Improving your self-esteem is probably the one most valuable activity you can undertake in preparation for a loving relationship.

There are lots of books, courses and seminars around which specialise in self-esteem work (see the back of this book for my personal recommendations). These are worth the investment of time and money.

What Does Love Mean, Anyway?

You have looked at the beliefs you have held in the past about yourself.

Now it is time to take a look at your beliefs about relationships.

EXERCISE

Take some more sheets of paper (yes, more!) and write the following statement:

"What love means to me is..." and complete the sentence with the first thing that comes into your mind.

Continue to write the phrase again and again, completing the sentence each time with whatever comes into your thoughts.

Here is an example of how it might go:

What love means to me is... red hearts.

What love means to me is... sex.

What love means to me is... sleeping with someone.

What love means to me is feeling helpless.

What love means to me is being out of control.

What love means to me is feeling scared.

What love means to me is being hurt. It reminds me of waking up alone in the morning.

What love means to me is pain.

You can get to some really interesting "bottom lines" with this exercise.

During this process you may start to remember experiences from your past that caused you to associate love with other emotions or certain people or events. You will begin to see where these beliefs originated.

Of course, the memories may be pleasant and happy.

But how many of us link *love* with *pain*? How many songs have we heard on the radio that talk about being *in love* and *hurting* all in one lyric? How many movies are about star-crossed lovers or lovers who have to go through a lot of misunderstanding and emotional pain before they can be happy together? *I love you so much it hurts...you've broken my heart...it hurts so good...*

Has love been painful for you? Do you believe that pain is inevitable? What if you are wrong? What if love does not *have* to be painful? I can assure you, it isn't for everyone. Would you like it to be different from now on? Wouldn't you like a choice?

Let's find out some of your other beliefs associated with relationships.

Here are some for you to play around with, in the same way as you did with the word "love".

What marriage means to me is...

What being a woman/man means to me is...

What sex means to me is...

What relationships mean to me is...

What men/women mean to me is...

What commitment means to me is...

What children mean to me is...

As you can see, these are all things that are related in some way to being in an intimate relationship. Find out your beliefs and associations with these words. Can you begin to see why, even though you truly want to be in a happy relationship, you may also be in conflict about it?

What fears have you discovered? It is possible that on the one hand your intention is to live happily with your ideal partner. On the other hand your intention may be to protect yourself from these fears and possible pain.

Fears: Fact Or Fiction?

But my fears are legitimate, you may say! I really *did* get hurt, it really *was* painful, my relationships really *are* always disasters!

Most of our adult relationships have been built upon the model we learned from our parents (or whoever took care of us when we were children).

Put simply, if our parents had a happy, healthy relationship, then we will probably grow up to have happy, healthy relationships of our own. If our parents' relationship was unhappy or destructive, then it is likely that we also will experience this kind of relationship as an adult.

Also, we acquire our first beliefs about ourselves from our parents (how worthy we are, how lovable) and this sets up a "blue-print" for how we expect to be treated as we grow into adults and begin adult relationships.

So, to a large extent, our adult relationships are a reflection of the models we learned as a child about ourselves and about relationships.

These models will have been modified as we grew up and acquired new information, of course, but the basic model will still be there. This is why it seems that sometimes we have no control over the type of relationship we get ourselves into, even if the adult part of us *knows* it is not good for us. (Do you keep falling in love with jealous men or bitchy women, as if you "can't help it"?)

It is as if the "child" part of us, who learned the first lessons about relationships and its own worthiness, is choosing our partners and conducting our relationships for us!

So, to change the pattern of our relationships, we need to first discover what that *child's* expectations are from its early life experiences.

EXERCISE

Firstly, think about your parents and their relationship together. Were they happy? Did they fight? Did they get divorced? Were they affectionate and demonstrative? Did one dominate the other? Was there any abuse - did they treat each other badly?

In other words, what sort of model were you given about male-female relationships? Perhaps you come from a single parent home or perhaps one of your parents walked out on the family. Perhaps one of your parents died when you were young. Perhaps one of your parents was an alcoholic, and caused misery to the whole family. Perhaps you grew up *without* parents, learning about male-female relationships from someone else.

Write down, in point form or at length, what you can remember about the relationships around you when you were a child.

Notes: _____

_____
_____
_____
_____
_____
_____
_____
_____
_____
_____

Now think back to your own relationship with each of your parents. What can you remember? How far back can you remember? Did you "get on" better with one parent than the other? Was one parent away working a lot of the time so you did not get to see him/her very much? Did your parents treat you with love and respect, or were you criticised and blamed?

Obstacles & How To Overcome Them

Write down details of your relationship with each of your parents, or the adults in your life who took care of you as you were growing up.

Notes: _____

_____
_____
_____
_____
_____
_____
_____
_____
_____
_____
_____
_____

Now think about each of your parents individually. What were they like? What sort of personalities did they have? How did they behave? What were some of their attitudes - especially to love, sex, marriage and their partner? How was their self-esteem?

Notes: _____

_____
_____

_____
_____
_____
_____
_____
_____
_____

Compare your own adult life, especially your adult relationships, to the notes you have taken. Can you see any similarities between the "love life" of your parents and your own love life? *Their* personalities and self-esteem and *your own* self-esteem?

This does not mean that the details need be exactly the same (although they could be - such as alcoholism being a recurring pattern, or physical violence), but rather that the emotional outcomes will be similar.

An example: A mother makes it her role in life to support her husband's career by taking care of the home. She puts aside her brushes and paints (which is the hobby she loves and for which she has a real talent) to iron his shirts, make his meals, bring up the children.

Her daughter decides early on that obviously a man is more important than a woman and a "good" woman should sacrifice her own needs.

It is now the "done thing" for young women to have ambition, so she grows up with her own career as a graphic artist. She finds this rewarding and fulfilling.

Then she meets a man and falls in love. Her career involvement means that she cannot be with him as much as he (or she) wants.

Obstacles & How To Overcome Them

So she begins to leave work early, leaving jobs unfinished or finished badly and she gives up her hobbies so that she can be with him. Before you know it she has the urge to iron his shirts (even though she hates ironing).

Another example: A woman with a small son is first abused and then deserted by her husband. She is relieved, and starts meeting other men. However, each man she meets either treats her badly, or goes out with her a few times and then does not call any more. The woman is very hurt and upset about these short-lived, unhappy relationships.

Her son decides early on that this is the way women are treated by men. He also feels very sorry and sad for his mother.

When he grows up, the son is a playboy. He goes out with lots of women who fall in love with him, but he dates them only a few times each, because he starts to feel uncomfortable and uneasy if he sees them for too long. The funny thing is, the more attracted he is to a woman, the more irritated he feels by her. He has never actually hit a woman, but sometimes he feels like giving just a little shove... then he feels terrible remorse and guilt about it, and ends the relationship in a hurry. He just stops returning calls. He wonders if he will ever find the love of his life and settle down.

The two examples above show how children learn a pattern of relationships and, even when they try to break away from it, they are drawn back to the habit or pattern. This is what they are used to. Habits are comfortable, even if logic says they are not good for us.

People also become used to being treated badly by others. Some people even feel uncomfortable being treated *well*. They cannot bear to be loved too much, and will even choose a cruel suitor over a loving one. It's ironic - they feel safer with an abusive partner, because the scenario matches their belief about themselves: that they are not worthy of anything better.

I know I seem to have been emphasising the *negative* side of relationships, and it is true that we not only learn destructive and hurtful things about ourselves and about relationships. We also learn positive, healthy things.

However it is not the positive side which is our obstacle to a happy fulfilling relationship.

It is the negative, unsupportive beliefs we want to change, so that we are free to choose the shape and direction of our future love life, rather than be at the mercy of our past patterns and habits.

In the exercises you have just completed *(examining and making notes about your childhood)*, you will have become aware of some of these past patterns and habits.

You will probably have discovered ways in which you, as an adult, have behaved in a similar way to one or other of your parents. You may have realised how much alike you are in some respects, and how you have unwittingly repeated some of their mistakes.

In gaining this awareness, you may feel angry or resentful towards your parents for "teaching you" some of these unhappy beliefs about yourself *(your worthiness, your lovability, for example)* and about relationships *(marriage is bondage, love is pain, for example)*.

EXERCISE

Complete the *Forgiveness Exercise* with each of your parents. Once again, this exercise is for your own benefit, not that of your parents, although if it improves your relationship with your parents, all to the good.

By forgiving your parents, you allow yourself to let go of the past hurts (no parent is perfect, just as you are not!), and also to begin to let go of those old patterns and habits of thinking about yourself and relationships.

Positive Affirmations

Now that you've explored some of your old negative beliefs, what do you do with them? You certainly don't want to hold on to them!

These negative beliefs were acquired by hearing and seeing them over and over again until they seemed like truth or fact. This same principle can be used in your favour: by hearing and seeing *positive* beliefs over and over again, until *they* seem like truth or fact. You can virtually flush out old negative beliefs by replacing them with a flood of opposite positive statements. These are commonly called affirmations, and they play a very powerful role in attracting what you desire.

EXERCISE

Below are some general positive affirmations for you to use, in addition to any you feel are specially suitable to yourself. Repeat the statements over and over to yourself at every opportunity: write them, or say them out loud or silently to yourself. The most effective time to do this is when you are relaxed, particularly upon waking or just before you go to sleep at night.

I am meeting the right partner.
I am happily married.
I am attracting a wonderful relationship.

Repeating significant single words can also be very effective: "love", "marriage", "intimacy", "tenderness", etc.

Review

In this section of the book you have achieved a greater awareness of your own beliefs about yourself and about relationships, and about how these beliefs, sparked long ago, have helped to shape your relationship history up until now.

This greater awareness, and willingness to let go of those beliefs which are not supportive of you having a fulfilling, lasting relationship and replacing them with beliefs which *are* supportive means that you have greater choice when it comes to

- creating a lasting relationship, and
- making sure that it is healthy, happy and positive.

This means that you are more free than ever before to pick and choose exactly the kind of relationship, and the kind of partner, you want.

You have worked hard during this section. Persevering with the exercises has taken commitment and time. Well done!

In the next section of the book (which is also the most fun part) you will be taking the information you have acquired so far and putting it to good use constructing your *Relationship Checklist*.

Part Four

Your Relationship Checklist

Your Relationship Checklist

The Power Of List Writing

There is great power in writing a list for something you want.

It forces you to become very clear about what you want.

From that *clarity* comes the *commitment* to having what you want, rather than some compromise.

It is *commitment* that has the *power* to create or attract what you want, sometimes in ways which seem miraculous.

"..the moment one commits oneself providence moves too. All sorts of things occur to help one that would never otherwise have occurred. A whole stream of events issues from the decision, raising in one's favour all manner of unforeseen incidents and meetings and material assistance which no man/woman could have dreamed would come their way."

W. H. Murray

I had been using the principles of clarity and commitment long before I applied them to finding my ideal relationship.

I would make detailed lists for things I wanted (such as jobs or accommodation) and, as the method proved itself time and time again, I became more and more daring with my lists.

I remember one time when I needed to move house with my daughter. I could not afford to rent alone, I did not have a car and I did not want to change my daughter's daycare mother, so I was rather limited in my options. I decided to put the "list method" to a serious test!

This is the list I wrote:

To share a house with another mother

Maximum rent $...

A house with a garden (but not a terrace - I hate them), located within five minutes "unhilly" walk of my daughter's daycare mother (I was still pushing a pram in those days!)

Within five minutes' walk of public transport to the city where I worked

New kitchen and bathroom (this was stretching it, since houses within five minutes' walk of the daycare mother were all very old)

Dry and free of mould (this was stretching it even more, since the suburb was notorious for its damp)

Large sunny rooms, freshly painted

Three bedrooms, or two bedrooms with sunroom

Private, quiet surroundings

Friendly neighbours with nice children

Clothesline and laundry.

Once I had finished the list, I began to have doubts: perhaps this time I was being unreasonably demanding. I reviewed the list and decided that yes, it really *was* my ideal. So I decided to stick with it.

Within a few days I had met a woman with a five-year-old son who was looking for a place to live.

Within a week I had found the place I was looking for.

It was a brand new self-contained house built in the back yard of an existing house (no terrace house, brand new everything, not just kitchen and bathroom, no damp, freshly painted). It was located - you guessed it - five minutes' unhilly walk from both daycare and public transport to the city. Being built at the back of a block, it was quiet and private. There was a garden, and a clothesline. It had three large sunny bedrooms, and the rent was slightly less than my allowed maximum. The next-door neighbour was a delightful woman with a lovely little boy.

The only thing I was not totally happy with was that it had polished wood floors instead of carpets, but guess who forgot to write *carpeted floors* on the list! I had assumed the floors would be carpeted.

The Relationship Checklist

I learned a good lesson from those polished floors: when writing a list, *never assume,* and *be specific!*

By the time I got around to writing a list of my ideal relationship, I had learned to write lists which were extremely detailed and specific, and which avoided any ambiguity, vagueness or assumptions. I made sure they were clear.

This process took quite a bit of soul-searching on my part. I had to find out exactly what it was that I wanted before I could achieve the *clarity* that would produce the *commitment* to have the *power* to create/attract what I wanted.

It paid off, because the extremely "fussy" list I wrote for the relationship I wanted attracted my husband, Les. When I went back to my list to "check it off" he matched it perfectly! I was astounded! There was not a *single thing* that I had asked for that I did not get.

In a way, I have been asking you to do your own soul-searching, because all the exercises in this book up until this point have been designed to help you achieve the all-important first step: *clarity* about what you truly want.

The Constructive Fantasising exercises will have assisted you to be detailed and specific in your list, writing for what you want in your love life, because you will have already identified some of the feelings and events you want to experience.

The section on "Obstacles" will have helped you to identify old beliefs and avoid making assumptions about what will make you happy in your love life, because you will have already become aware of any destructive patterns that you don't wish to repeat.

Checklist Categories

This list you are going to write will really "spell it out" when it comes to what kind of partner and what kind of relationship you want to attract into your life.

To make it easier for you, I have listed some categories (lots, actually!) of everyday areas of your life with a partner. Just take one category at a time, and describe what you want concerning that area of your relationship.

By the time you have come to the end of the categories, you will have a powerful list and a great deal of clarity about what you want.

Many of these categories may surprise you. Several you will not even have thought about before at all.

Isn't Love Enough?

Some of you may think: isn't this amount of detail a little unnecessary? Surely love is enough?

Well, loving each other will get you a long way. However, most couples these days love each other when they marry, but it doesn't stop up to 40% of them also *getting divorced!*

It is the *small* things that can make or break a relationship. A lot of small incompatibilities can add up to irritation... intolerance... arguments... alienation...

Taking care of the small compatibilities also avoids one fatal mistake that many, many people (dare I say *most*) make at some time in their relationship history.

That is, getting involved with someone for their *potential* and hoping they'll change or grow or "become someone".

This does not work, ladies and gentlemen. *No, no, no!*

True, people *do* change. But they change because they *choose* to change, not because someone else wants them to change. So it is very risky to base your involvement on the hope that your partner will become something they are not. They may, and then again *they may not*.

A big part of a successful relationship is an attitude of unconditional love and acceptance.

That is, you love your partner for who they are *right now*, not for what they *might become*. You will love them even if they remain exactly as they are for the rest of their lives.

So if there are things that are important to you to have in a relationship, *list them now* - better to have them be part of your partner when you meet.

A simple example is *smoking*. If you are a non-smoker and would complain or nag your partner to give it up, don't get involved with a smoker in the first place. Why put yourself (and your partner) through it? Write *"non-smoker"* on your list.

Describing your relationship category by category in as much detail as possible will make your relationship as *real* to you as possible. And the more you can imagine your relationship in terms of everyday events, the more powerfully you can attract that person into your life.

Don't be afraid that you are being too fussy (remember my "impossible" house).

Nothing is too much to ask. You deserve the best.

Remember, the more specific you are (that is, the more "choosy") the more powerful the ability to attract what you want.

Anyway, try it. You are bound to get excited as your ideal partner seems to come to life before you on the page.

Notes: _____

Guidelines

- Tell the story of your ideal relationship as if it already exists.

For example, instead of writing:

"I want the relationship between my partner and me to be loving and peaceful and I would prefer us to share some hobbies"

write:

"The relationship between my partner and me is loving and peaceful. We share some hobbies."

In the first example the relationship sounds like a future wish, whereas in the second example it sounds as if it is *real, now*.

- Describe your partner and relationship in a positive way.

For example, instead of writing:

"My partner is not bad-tempered or cruel. He never hits me"

write:

"My partner is good-natured. He is kind and gentle to me."

It is a good idea to steer clear of negative descriptions if you can, because your mind will register the negative words and remind you of things you don't really want to focus on. If I say to you *"don't think of an elephant!"*, what do you think of? An *elephant*, of course!

Describing positively instead of negatively can be difficult at first. Many of us know very clearly (from bitter experience) what we *don't* want, and the tendency is to write things like: *"I don't want a woman who is bitchy or jealous, or who smokes and drinks a lot. She must not run around with other men or nag me into doing things I don't want to do"*.

If this happens to you, take a separate sheet of paper and write down all the things you don't want in your partner or relationship. Then re-write them in a positive way. This can be a challenge, and if you get stuck just think how fixed your mind has been on those negative qualities!

(A "translation" of the above example could go something like this:

"My partner is loving and trusting. She is a moderate drinker. She is romantically interested only in me and is happy for me to do the things that make me happy." It sounds much better, doesn't it?)

- Not all the categories I have listed will necessarily apply to you or interest you.

You can skip over these altogether, if you like. The categories I have listed are just a guide to help you. You may also want to include some areas I have not mentioned at all.

However, don't ignore some just because you haven't ever thought about this area of your own life before. Perhaps, rather than it not being important, you just *don't know* what you want in this area of your relationship.

Stop and think about it for a while. Do some more Constructive Visualisation.

For example, in the category "Holidays" - perhaps you have been so pre-occupied with your career that you have never even taken holidays. Now you are being asked to describe the kind of holidays *you and your partner* take! Stop. Imagine you are in that wonderful relationship. Close your eyes. Fantasise. Do you want to take the time away from your work to holiday with your partner? Where would you go? What kind of atmosphere would your holiday place have? Or would your partner be quite happy to give up holidays so you could continue your work (or vice versa)?

If you are still unsure, perhaps you need to find out more about what kind of holiday you would like to take for *yourself*. Get more information. Buy travel magazines. Get some brochures from a tourist bureau.

You may find out a lot about yourself during this exercise, because in the process of describing your ideal partner and relationship you are challenged to examine *your own* preferences, values, likes and dislikes.

If in doubt, you can just be general and write something like:

"My partner and I have compatible opinions and preferences about ...."

Finally, really *let yourself go* with this exercise. Relationships are about feelings and emotions, so use words that really mean something to you. You can be as romantic as you want, using all the mushy words you want. No-one else is ever going to know unless you tell them. Whatever makes it real for you.

Or if writing isn't your "thing", you can write your list in point form.

The important thing is to allow yourself to get excited about the partner and the relationship you are "creating" because this excitement and energy contributes greatly to the power to attract what you want.

EXERCISE

Take one category at a time and start writing your relationship list. I have given some prompts in each category to assist you.

Your Relationship Together

Type of Relationship

Marriage, living together? How long does the relationship last? Is it peaceful, passionate, supportive, fun, productive, harmonious?

_____
_____
_____
_____

Feelings Between Us

How do you feel about your partner? How does your partner feel about you? What do you think of each other (eg approve, respect)? How do you treat each other (in private, in public)? How do you feel about yourself when you are with your partner (eg desirable, intelligent) and how does your partner feel when around you?

_____
_____
_____
_____
_____
_____
_____

Your Relationship Checklist

Compatibility

In what areas of your life are you compatible (eg spiritual, mental, physical, emotional)?

Note: Compatibility doesn't mean that you have to be exactly the same as each other. It means that you are able to exist together in harmony. It basically means how *easy* your relationship is together and how well you handle life's little challenges and setbacks together.

_____
_____
_____
_____
_____
_____
_____
_____
_____
_____
_____
_____
_____
_____
_____
_____
_____
_____
_____

Your Partner - Attitudes & Characteristics

Life Values

Morals, priorities, ambitions, prejudices (or not), optimism/pessimism

_____
_____
_____
_____

Relationship Values

Beliefs, personal standards (eg. honesty, caring, jealousy, freedom, possessiveness, fidelity, trust). It also includes beliefs about roles in the relationship: who does what around the home, with the children, income-earning.

_____
_____
_____
_____

Interests and Hobbies

Is it important that you share these? Which ones?

_____
_____
_____
_____

Lifestyle and Location

Country cottage or city apartment? Crystal goblets or tin camping mugs? Or both?

_____

_____

_____

Money

What is your partner's attitude to money (eg miser, generous)? Is it important or not?

_____

_____

Work

Workaholic or "work to live"?

_____

_____

_____

Play and Fun

What does fun mean to your partner? How do you "play" in your lives together?

_____

_____

_____

Religion/Spirituality

Important or not, beliefs, activities, involvement etc.

_____

_____

_____

Politics

Important or not, beliefs, involvement etc.

_____

_____

Marital Status

Is it okay if your partner has been previously married, divorced, widowed?

_____

_____

Romance

Is your partner romantic? Is it important? Your partner's definition of romance (eg dinner in a top restaurant or popcorn in front of the television).

_____

_____

_____

_____

Humour

What brand of humour (slapstick, intellectual, crude and rude)? Is it important?

_____

_____

Children

Beliefs about parenting, kids or no kids, kids from past relationships, wants them, likes them, not important? If your partner has children from a previous relationship, what is your relationship like with them? Is it important? If you have children of your own, what is your partner's relationship with them?

_____

_____

_____

Nature and the Outdoors

If you're a serious greenie and your partner hates the outdoors and refuses to recycle… is this important?

_____

_____

Pets

Is a love of animals important?

_____

_____

Holidays

Does your partner take holidays with you? What type? How often? Is it important?

_____
_____
_____
_____

Friends

Are mutual friends important? Do you share some? Do you like your partner's friends, and vice versa?

_____
_____
_____
_____

Entertainment

Tastes in music, sport, movies, books, dining. What constitutes "a good time" for your partner? Is it important it is the same as yours?

_____
_____
_____
_____
_____

Time Together

Do you need lots of solitude? What if your partner wants to spend every waking moment in your company?

_____
_____
_____
_____
_____
_____

Health, Fitness and Food

Is this important? If one of you is a fitness fanatic and the other is a slob, does this matter? What if you're into salads and freshly squeezed juices and your partner's into burgers and coke?

_____
_____
_____
_____

Personal Habits

Drugs, gambling, alcohol, smoking

_____
_____
_____
_____

Communication

Is your partner the "strong, silent type" or a talker? How do you communicate with each other?

_____
_____
_____

Sex and Touching

What kind of lover is your partner? Describe your sex life.

_____
_____
_____

Background, Career, Nationality and Age

Are any of these important to you?

_____
_____
_____

Personal Style

What if one of you is a strictly jeans and t-shirt type and the other wants to do the town in tuxedo or furs?

_____
_____
_____

Appearance

You may wish to describe some physical ideal (*tall, dark, handsome* or *blonde, big breasts, model figure*).

However, successful relationships are not based on physical beauty. What *is* important is that you find your partner attractive - even better, *irresistible!*

I suggest you describe your ideals as *preferences*, not *essentials*. You may just get them! On the other hand, is it really important whether or not your partner is a classic stunner as long as you absolutely adore each other?

_____
_____
_____
_____
_____

This is not an exhaustive list (believe it or not!)

You may have thought of areas not mentioned, but which are significant or personal to you.

The point is to tell a story, paint a picture, create a feeling of the relationship you truly want.

Have some fun with this, focusing on what you most want to *experience* in your relationship.

Write your story in the present tense, making it as vivid as possible, because engaging your own emotions is one of the most powerful factors involved in attracting what you want into your life.

Your needs may change over time, particularly as you improve your relationship with yourself: increasing your self-esteem, loving and caring for yourself a lot more and getting to know yourself better.

Generally speaking, the better your relationship with yourself and the more able you are to meet your own needs (for approval, security, resassurance), the less dependant you will be on (and the less demanding of) your partner to meet those needs for you. Your criteria for what kind of partner will make you happy may have changed.

So review your list from time to time.

Notes: _____

Part Five

Next Steps

Next Steps

Congratulations! You have made it this far!

You will have a greater understanding of yourself and your needs for loving relationships - with yourself, others and a special "other".

You will have begun to let go of old relationships, beliefs and patterns which were destructive or limiting.

You will have imagined what it is like to be in a happy, healthy relationship, and you will have a clear idea of what is going to make you happy.

You have written a detailed list of what you want in a partner and in a relationship.

So, what's next?

Commitment

The power of your list to attract what you want comes from your commitment to it.

If you start compromising your ideal, it loses power.

It takes faith and belief in yourself that you deserve the best, not *second* best.

Perhaps you meet a charming smoker, and are tempted to compromise your wish for a non-smoker. Your mind can be very persuasive: *"It's not that important, he/she may give it up..."*.

Only include those specifics which are *really important* to you.

Review your list from time to time, as you become clearer about what will make you happy in a partner and in a relatationship.

Be *devoted* to your goal.

Be Available

If you compromise and start a relationship with *second* best, you will not be available for the *best*.

Starting a "in the meantime while I'm waiting for my ideal" kind of relationship will not necessarily prevent your ideal coming along, but it sure will make it more complicated, and you risk hurting yourself, your "temporary" partner *and* your future partner.

If a relationship you are in at the moment is obviously not the ideal you hope for, then either work on the relationship to give it a chance to become your ideal (by doing the exercises in this book you may clear away old beliefs and hurts which are making a current relationship unhappy) *or* do the compassionate thing (for both of you) and bring the relationship to a close.

Circulate

Make room for the relationship to come into your life!

This does not necessarily mean you have to change your lifestyle by taking up new hobbies or joining clubs or visiting places you would not normally be seen.

Also, if you have been meeting people through introduction agencies, singles parties, clubs, groups or through magazine contact there is no reason to discontinue these methods. They can be legitimate ways of meeting eligible partners.

However, it *does* mean having an attitude of *"I like people... I am nice to be with... relationships of all kinds are important to me... I make time for people in my life."*

This kind of attitude is attractive to others. People will want to be around you. You will make new friends and expand your social circle.

So your future partner will have the chance to find you!

Fantasise, Fantasise, Fantasise!

Continue to imagine yourself already in your future relationship.

Think about your day-to-day life: how would your partner fit into it? Imagine having conversations, dinners, outings, going shopping... imagine how it would feel to have a constant companion.

You can do your fantasising sitting down by yourself and closing your eyes, or you can stop at any time during your day and imagine what it would be like if your partner was with you *at that moment*.

For example, if you are at the movies by yourself or with friends, imagine what it would be like if the love of your life was suddenly seated beside you! Would you be holding hands, snuggling up, eating popcorn, giggling and making a disturbance? How would it feel?

Have fun with fantasising!

Be The Best You Can Be

Start living up to your list!

If you want a partner who is loving, a good friend, honest, affectionate and giving, ask yourself: *"Do I practise what I preach?"* Someone who has the qualities you are looking for is probably also going to want to meet someone with those qualities, too. How do you measure up to your own list?

If you want to be loved, then *be loving* to others and to yourself. If you want someone who is a good friend, then *be a good friend*. If you want someone who is honest, affectionate and giving, then *be honest and affectionate and giving*.

If trust is important to you, then practise *being trustworthy and trusting*. If you want respect, then *show respect* of yourself and others.

Make the most of yourself. Be prepared: what if you are going to meet your future partner *tomorrow?*

Do you have doubts about your own attractiveness?

"Attractive" means different things to different people (thank goodness!). That's why in your list I suggest you write "attractive to me" rather than specific features such as hair or eye colour.

Often our preconceived ideas of "beauty" change from an emphasis on external features when we see that special inner spark of a loved one. Ever loved a stray dog or a mangy cat?

Have you ever seen a couple and commented *"What does she see in him?"* or *"What can he possibly find attractive in her?"*. As they say, looks aren't everything.

On the other hand, do the best you can with what you've got. If you are unsure how you can make the most of what you've got, ask a trusted friend or a professional (hairdresser/beautician/wardrobe adviser/health and fitness practitioner) for some advice.

And then there's the simple things like smelling nice, being clean and wearing a smile.

There is nothing wrong with putting some icing on the basically already beautiful cake which is *you*.

Relax! & Love Yourself

Relax! How long you take to attract your ideal partner depends on how much time and work you are prepared to devote to yourself and your own happiness.

It's up to you to make yourself and your desire for a happy, healthy relationship important enough to do whatever it takes. For as long as it takes!

If the ideas and exercises in this book have been fairly new to you, you may want to look at this book as the beginning of your journey towards your ideal relationship - first with yourself, then with another.

The most important single factor when it comes to attracting love is *having a loving attitude* - to life, to others and especially to yourself.

The most important relationship is the one you have with yourself. Treat yourself well, and other people will treat you well too.

Build your self-esteem. Do courses. Read books.

Continue the simple self-esteem exercises from Part Three of this book.

Practise applying the techniques to other, perhaps less emotionally important areas of your life to build up your confidence in your ability to attract what you want, such as jobs, houses, flatmates, friends, etc.

You don't get what you deserve in this life. You get what you *think* you deserve...

...and that includes your love life.

Recommended Reading & Further Study

Books

The Power Of Your Subconscious Mind by Dr Joseph Murphy. Published by Simon & Schuster 1963.

One-Minute Self-Esteem by Candy Semigran. Published by Insight Publishing 1988.

Creative Visualisation by Shakti Gawain. Published by Bantam Books 1978.

Affirmations by Stuart Wilde. Published by White Dove International, Inc. 1987.

Seminars

Insight Seminars, conducted in Australia and numerous countries around the world.

There are many excellent books, courses and seminars on the subjects of self-esteem, relationships, the power